CRAFT TOPICS

FLAGS

FACTS ● THINGS TO MAKE ● ACTIVITIES

Chris Oxlade
Illustrated by Raymond Turvey

Franklin Watts
A Division of Grolier Publishing
New York ● London ● Hong Kong ● Sydney
Danbury, Connecticut

© 1995 Franklin Watts

Franklin Watts
95 Madison Avenue
New York, NY 10016

Editor: Annabel Martin
Designed by: Sally Boothroyd
Photography by: Martyn Chillmaid
Additional picture research by: Veneta Bullen

Library of Congress Cataloging-in-Publication Data

Oxlade, Chris.
    Flags / by Chris Oxlade.
      p.   cm.   - (Craft Topics)
    Includes bibliographical references and index.
    ISBN 0-531-14386-4
    1. Flags-Juvenile literature.   I. Title.   II. Series.
    CR109.096   1995   95-11604
    929.9'2–dc20   CIP AC

Printed in the United Kingdom

CONTENTS

All about Flags   4
The Origin of Flags   6
Make a Vexillum   8
Flag Shapes and Designs   10
Heraldry and Arms   12
Make a 3-D Coat of Arms   14
Flags at Sea   16
Communicating with Flags   18
Flags in Battle   20
Some National Flags   22
Design and Make a Flag   24
International Flags   26
Using Flags   28
Glossary   30
Resources   31
Index   32

ALL ABOUT FLAGS

There are thousands of different flags in the world. Individual countries, kings and queens, companies, societies, and organizations such as armies and navies, have their own flags. Flags are also used for communication and sending messages, and for decoration. You can find out more about some types of flags below.

FOLLOW THE FLAG

Flags are flown on special days in a country's history. On the Fourth of July – Independence Day in the United States – the American flag is flown on every flagpole. People wave large and small national flags, and long strings of brightly colored flags, called bunting, are hung from buildings.

Left: *Flags flying from houses to celebrate Independence Day*

FLYING FLAGS

Flags are often painted on vehicles such as aircraft. They show that the aircraft belongs to the fleet of a particular country. Other national airlines use parts of the national flag for their insignia, if not the flag itself.

FLAGS IN SPACE

When the astronauts of Apollo 11 made the first landing on the moon in 1969, they set up the "Stars and Stripes," the flag of the United States, on the moon's surface. It showed that the United States was the first country to land men on the moon. Because there is no air on the moon, there is no wind, so the flag had to be supported by an extra staff along the top edge to make it hang correctly.

NEW FLAGS

Every so often, political boundaries are changed or redrawn, and a new country is formed. When this happens, a new national flag has to be designed. New flags are also designed when countries become independent from their old rulers, or when a new government takes power.

YOU WIN

Flags are also used to send messages. Some flags are known all over the world. One example is a plain white flag, which means truce, or "I surrender." It is used in war situations. A red flag is often flown to warn people of a dangerous hazard, such as a rifle range.

BANNERS

Not all flags fly on upright poles. Hanging flags, which are sometimes called banners, hang downward from horizontal poles or ropes. Long banners are popular in China. They are often used as shop signs which can be seen from far down the street.

THE ORIGIN OF FLAGS

Historians do not know exactly when the first flags were made, or who used them. The earliest flags did not look like the flags we are familiar with today, but they were used for the same purposes – to send signals and to identify the flag carrier.

SOLID FLAGS

Archaeologists have found evidence that flaglike objects were already being used about 4,000 years ago in China and Egypt. Like modern flags, these early flags were displayed on poles. However, they were not made of fabric, but were carved from wood. Decorative, brightly colored ribbons were sometimes tied to the poles as well.

Some Vikings also used flags that blew out in the wind. The flags were flown from the Vikings' longships as they raided the coasts of European countries between the ninth and eleventh centuries. The Raven flag had a figure of a black raven in the center.

FLAGS OF THE LEGIONS

Each unit of the Roman army had its own standard, used for identification. It was normally a wooden pole with a cloth square, various badges and medals attached to it. The most famous standards, which had a sculpted eagle at the top, belonged to the Roman legions. The medals were awarded for the legion's victories in battle. Some standards included a flag called a vexillum, which hung from a bar attached horizontally to the pole.

The vexillum was the first type of flag to look like the ones we know today. The study of flags is called vexillology after the vexillum.

A vexillum, a flag carried by mounted units of the Roman army.

A Roman draco

BLOWING IN THE WIND

Another type of Roman flag was called a draco, which means "dragon." It was a hollow, dragon-shaped tube that billowed out in the wind. It would have looked a bit like a modern wind sock. This was one of the first flags to use the wind to be displayed, as most modern flags do.

Make a Vexillum

A vexillum was the type of flag attached to the standard of a unit of the Roman army. It was made from a square of red cloth attached to a bar along its top edge. The flag might also have shown a badge that symbolized the unit, such as the running boar of the XXth Legion. A real vexillum was more elaborate than the model shown below, with a gold fringe and silver-tipped ribbon.

You will need: ● string ● small saw ● aluminum foil ● thick cardboard ● colored fabric or construction paper ● wooden dowels (thick and thin) ● needle and thread or glue ● fabric paints or poster paints

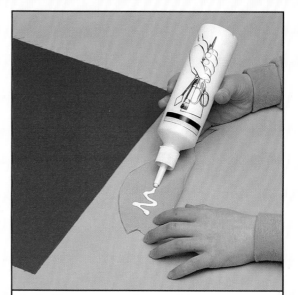

▲ **2.** If you are making a fabric vexillum, paint the symbols using fabric paint, or cut shapes from a different colored cloth and sew or glue them in place. If you are making a cardboard vexillum, paint the symbols or glue on cardboard shapes.

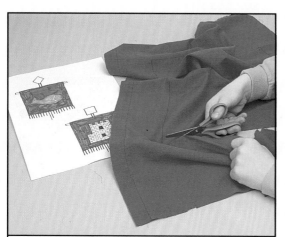

▲ **1.** Start by making some sketches of the symbols you want to put on your vexillum. When you have a design you like, cut a rectangle of fabric or construction paper. Make it at least 12 inches (30 cm) wide. Make the height about 2 inches (5 cm) more than the width.

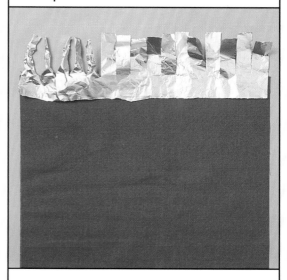

▲ **3.** Cut thin strips of aluminum foil and roll them up. Glue them to the back of the vexillum along the bottom to make a frill.

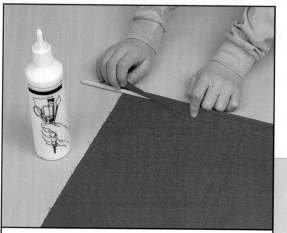

4. Cut a length of a thin wooden dowel about 4 inches (10 cm) longer than your vexillum's width. Lay your vexillum face down, hold the dowel across the top, and fold the cloth or cardboard over the dowel. Glue it down.

5. Cut a piece of thick dowel between 5 and 6 feet (1.5 and 2 m) long for the pole. Make a finial (a decoration for the top of the pole) by gluing aluminum foil to a piece of cardboard and cutting out a pointed shape. Glue it to the top of the pole. Finally, tie the vexillum to the pole with string.

FLAG SHAPES AND DESIGNS

Most modern flags are rectangular, but flags come in different shapes as well. Many flags, especially national flags, share similar design but have different colors. Each part of a flag has its own special name, as do the parts of the flagpole.

MODERN FLAG SHAPES

Most rectangular flags are longer than they are high. But some are tall and thin, and others are square.

A swallowtail flag is a rectangular flag (above) with a v-shaped piece cut out at the end to give it a shape like a swallow's forked tail.

Triangular flag

A pennant is a long triangular flag. A pennant has a bar at one end to keep it in shape, and hangs by a cord. Some pennants are also mounted on a vertical pole, like ordinary flags.

TECHNICAL TERMS

Almost every part of a flag has a special name. The most important ones are shown on this diagram.

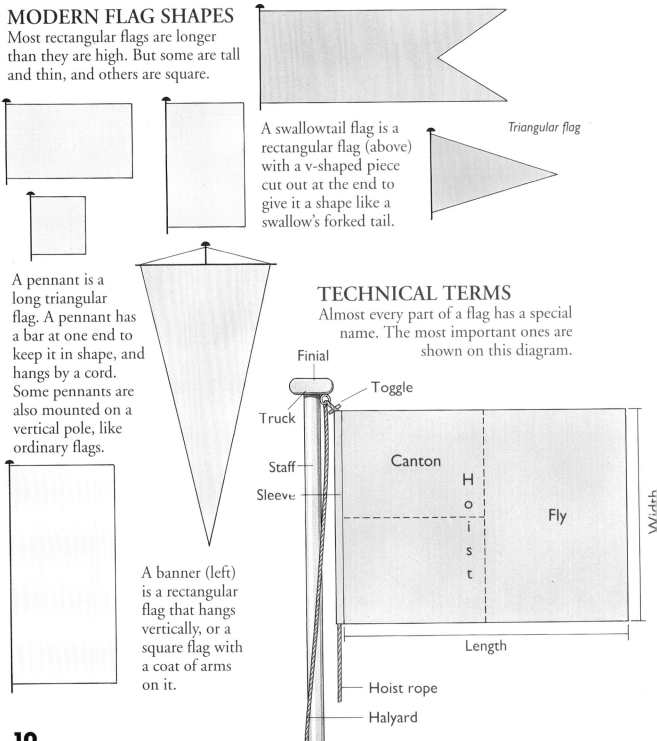

Finial

Toggle

Truck

Canton

Staff

Sleeve

H
o
i
s
t

Fly

Width

Length

Hoist rope

Halyard

A banner (left) is a rectangular flag that hangs vertically, or a square flag with a coat of arms on it.

COMMON DESIGNS

There are hundreds of different flag designs, divided into different groups that share similar features. The tricolor design with three stripes in different colors is very common. Many flags have a design in the upper hoist canton (the top quarter of the flag nearest the flagpole).

PROJECT: MAKE A PENNANT

A pennant is a popular shape for a sports club flag. Club pennants are often exchanged between club teams before matches. Try making a pennant for the club you belong to or support.

You will need: ● wooden dowels ● colored construction paper or thin cardboard ● colored felt-tip markers or paints ● string ● glue ● thumbtacks

2. Cut a piece of dowel a bit longer than the width of your pennant. Lay it along the top of the pennant. Fold the cardboard over the dowel and glue it in place. Put thumbtacks in the end of the dowel and tie on a length of string.

▲ **1.** First, design your pennant. The pennant should include the club emblem and some other decoration. Make a few sketches before deciding which one you like best. Cut the pennant shape from cardboard. Draw the design in pencil before coloring it with pens or paint.

HERALDRY AND ARMS

Many national and official flags have symbols and pictures on them that were designed hundreds of years ago. These symbols and pictures show that the flag belongs to a certain person such as a member of the royal family or an institution such as a city council. The art of designing and studying these symbols is called heraldry.

DECORATED SHIELDS

During the Middle Ages, knights began to decorate their large shields with symbols and pictures. When they began to wear helmets that covered their faces, the symbols on the shields were the only way of telling who the knight was during tournaments and battles. Special artists called herald-painters were responsible for decorating knights' shields.

A COAT OF ARMS

Gradually, each knight developed his own personal design for his shield. A picture of the shield was drawn on the coat that covered the knight's armor, and other symbols were added, such as animals holding the shield. The complete picture became known as a "coat of arms." The symbols in the coat of arms were soon arranged on a flag called a standard. The standard showed the knight's colors, badges and motto, and was flown at his castle. Another flag, called a banner, was carried by a horseman who rode with the knight.

The knight's shield and banner show his coat of arms

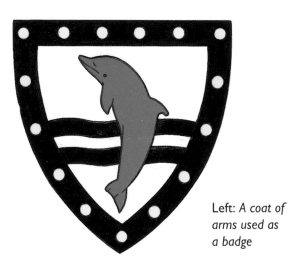

PASS IT ON

Only the knight himself was allowed to use his coat of arms. When he died, his heir took it over. Coats of arms were passed down from generation to generation. Many people still have coats of arms that look just as they did in the Middle Ages. People are also able to commission their own new coats of arms if they wish. Other organizations, such as colleges, companies, and trade unions developed their own coats of arms. Coats of arms can also be used as badges and buttons, and on seals, and documents.

Right: *The arms of Cornwall, England*

Left: *A coat of arms used as a badge*

MAKE A 3-D COAT OF ARMS

Coats of arms are sometimes made into three-dimensional plaques that can be hung on the wall. You can find out how to design and make your own three-dimensional coat of arms plaque below.

You will need: ● newspaper
● wallpaper paste (fungicide free)
● thick cardboard or posterboard
● paints ● craft knife ● varnish

▲ **1.** First, design your coat of arms. Use your name or your hobbies as a starting point for ideas, and draw some emblems that relate to you. Make sketches to decide how to fit your emblems on your coat of arms. Also think about other decorations, such as borders. Decide which parts will be in 3-D.

▲ **3.** Using scissors, cut sheets of newspaper into small pieces (about $1/2$ inch [1 cm] square). Put the pieces into a bowl and stir in wallpaper paste to make pulp. Use the pulp to build up the shapes of your symbols on the shield.

▲ **2.** Cut a shield-shaped piece from thick cardboard or posterboard using a craft knife or saw. Ask an adult to help you with this. Copy your sketch onto the base.

▲ **4.** Let the pulp dry for a few days, and then paint the coat of arms. Varnish it to protect the paint.

FLAGS AT SEA

Sailors have used flags on their ships for hundreds of years, and most ships still carry a flag showing their country of origin. Flags were one of the most important ways of sending messages between ships before Morse code was invented in the mid 1800s.

ENSIGNS

Ships display a special version of the national flag of the country they come from. It is called an ensign. Some countries have different designs of ensign, one for naval ships, one for merchant ships, and one for ships on government duty. Ensigns are also flown by private boats and ships, such as yachts. Sometimes ensigns have extra badges added to them. For example, a yacht might fly an ensign with its yacht club badge in one corner. Ensigns are normally flown on a small flagpole at the stern (rear) of a ship.

JACKS AND COURTESY FLAGS

A jack is a flag flown at the bow (front) of a warship. The jack is usually different from the country's national flag. However the jack used on British ships is the same as the national flag, the Union Jack. When merchant ships and warships from one country dock in a port in another country, they also fly the flag of the country they are visiting. This is called a courtesy flag.

A warship anchored in a foreign port. It is flying its own jack and a courtesy flag

DRESSING SHIP

On special occasions such as coronation days or ceremonial days, crews often "dress ship." This means that they hoist all the flags on board in colorful rows. In the past, when flags were the main way of communicating at sea, the whole ship's rigging (the ropes used to hoist and control the sails) would disappear beneath a mass of flags.

SIGNALS AT SEA

Before Morse code and radio were invented, sailors on one ship often used flags to talk to sailors on another. Displaying a flag, such as an ensign, in a special way had a certain meaning. For example, flying the ensign upside down signaled distress. Ordinary flags were also used as part of the signaling system but were flown from unusual points on the ship or in combination with other flags. In the eighteenth century, numeral flags were invented. Each flag represented a numeral, and the flags were hoisted in groups to make up numbers. Some numbers stood for individual letters, some stood for whole words, and some for whole sentences. At the Battle of Trafalgar in 1805, Admiral Nelson used numeral flags to send his famous signal "England expects that every man will do his duty." You can see the modern flag code on the next pages.

COMMUNICATING WITH FLAGS

There are several different ways of communicating with flags. To send a worded message, you can use either the international code signal flags or semaphore flags. There are also many flags with their own special use, for example, at motor racing events.

INTERNATIONAL CODE FLAGS

There are 40 international code flags – one for each of the 26 letters of the alphabet, one for each numeral from 0 to 9, an answering flag, and three substitute flags. The substitute flags are used for letters when the flag for a particular letter has already been used. The international code flags are shown below.

SEND CODED MESSAGES TO A FRIEND

Using felt pens, carefully copy all the flags on to a piece of paper and give it to a friend. You can write coded messages to each other using the international flags.

If you prefer, use colored paper and glue to make paper copies of the flags, and signal secret messages to your friend across a room!

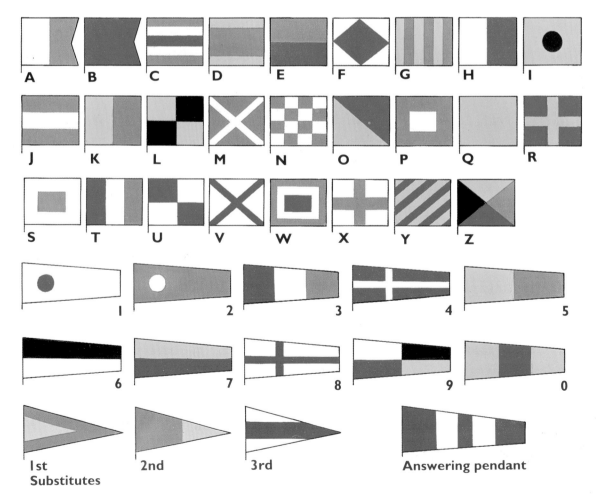

FLAGS IN SPORT

Flags are used to send messages in some sports. In soccer, the linesmen use their flags to show that the ball has gone out of play, or that a player has broken the rules in some way. The famous checkered flag in motor racing signals the end of the race. Track marshals can warn drivers of danger with yellow flags, or stop the race by waving red flags.

RED FOR DANGER

A red flag on its own often means danger. Red flags are flown on artillery ranges to warn people to stay back. A red flag at the coast often means that there are strong tides that would make swimming dangerous.

PROJECT: FLAG MESSAGES

You can send messages to your friends with international code flags. The flags will join together to make whole words. Or you could make up your own message flags.

▲ 1. Cut each flag shape from cardboard. Copy the designs from the list on these pages. Make one flag for each letter and number.

You will need: ● white cardboard or oaktag ● string ● glue ● colored pens or paints ● safety matches

2. Cut a piece of string twice as long as your flags. Tie a loop at one end and a matchstick to the other. Glue the string along the edge of the flag.

FLAGS IN BATTLE

In the past, soldiers going into battle carried flags to show which side they were on. Each unit of an army had its own flag, and so did each high-ranking officer. Even with modern communications, flags are still used as an easy and immediate way of identifying armored vehicles and military camps.

LANCE PENNONS

A pennon is a small flag in the shape of a swallow's tail. Cavalry soldiers always had a pennon near the end of their lances. Pennons have been used by armies all over the world for many hundreds of years. The Bayeux Tapestry shows cavalry soldiers with pennons fighting at the Battle of Hastings in 1066. Today, armored vehicles have taken the place of cavalry, but pennons are still used. They are flown from the radio aerials of tanks and armored cars.

Knights of the Middle Ages identified themselves by flying pennons and painting symbols on their shields

FLAGS FOR GROUPS

Until the sixteenth century, armies were not organized as they are today. A large army consisted of small groups of men fighting for their own particular master rather than for their king or country. When modern armies grew up, each unit had its own flag. The flag of a regiment became known as its regimental colors. Regimental colors are no longer carried into battle, but they are still an object of pride for the regiment.

The flag identifies the soldiers inside this armored car

A regiment displaying colors

KEEPING THE FLAG FLYING

A regiment's colors were important for keeping soldiers' spirits up. They were often carried by a flag bearer in the front line of battle. If the bearer was killed or injured, another soldier would pick up the colors. If a regiment's colors were captured by the enemy, the morale of the soldiers was badly damaged. National flags were just as important in battle. When an important town or hill was captured by an army, the national flag was hoisted to celebrate, and to show that the town or hill was controlled by that country's army.

SOME NATIONAL FLAGS

Certain colors or emblems are chosen for national flags because they mean something about the country they represent. This might have to do with a country's history, people, religion, or even countryside. Here are some examples from around the world.

THE UNITED KINGDOM

The national flag of the United Kingdom is known as the Union Jack. It is made up of the crosses of St. George, St. Andrew, and St. Patrick, the patron saints of England, Scotland, and Ireland.

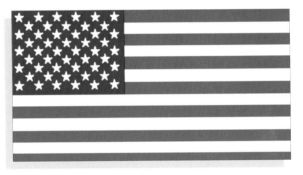

THE UNITED STATES

Because of its design, the flag of the United States is known as the "Stars and Stripes." There are fifty stars, one for each state today, and thirteen stripes, one for each of the original states that existed in 1777, when the flag was adopted.

AUSTRALIA

The Union Jack in the corner of the Australian flag shows Australia's historical links with Britain. The group of five stars at the end of the flag represents the Southern Cross, a bright constellation of stars which can be seen from the southern hemisphere.

FRANCE

The French national flag is known as the Tricolore (which means "three colors" in French). Red and blue were the colors of Paris and white was the color of the Bourbons, who were the royal family of France before the French Revolution.

GERMANY

Black, red, and gold were first used in the German flag in the early nineteenth century. The colors come from the uniforms of a regiment of soldiers who fought against Napoleon in the Napoleonic Wars. The modern flag has been in use since 1949, when East and West Germany were formed after World War II, but was also the official German flag from 1918 to 1933.

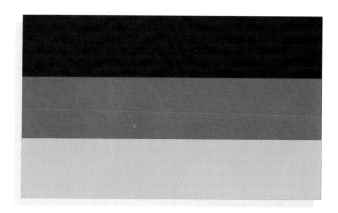

CANADA

The leaf in the center of the Canadian flag is a maple leaf of the red maple tree, which is common in Canada. Red and white are the heraldic colors of Canada. The flag was introduced in 1965.

CHINA

The present Chinese flag was designed in 1949 when the Communist party took over the country. The large star is the symbol of communism and the smaller stars stand for the four classes of people in Chinese society. Red is the color of communism.

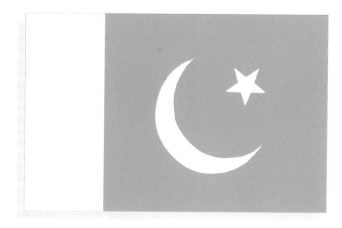

PAKISTAN

Pakistan was created in 1947 when India was divided into India and Pakistan. Its flag reflects the fact that the majority of its people are Muslims. Green is the traditional color of Islam, the religion of the Muslims, and the star and crescent moon are the traditional symbols.

DESIGN AND MAKE A FLAG

On these pages you can find out how to make your own flag and a flagpole to fly it from. You could make a copy of a national flag, or design your own flag in your favorite colors.

▲ **1.** Before you start making your flag, think about what you want it to look like. Experiment with the scraps of fabric and decide how many colors you want. Do you want a plain flag, a tricolor, or horizontal or vertical stripes? Make a full-scale sketch of your final design.

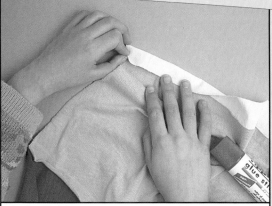

▲ **3.** Fold a narrow strip of fabric in half lengthwise to form a tube. Join the edges to the edge of the flag that will be nearest the flagpole.

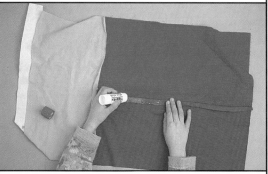

▲ **2.** Cut the stripes or other shapes for your flag from the scraps of fabric. Cut them about 1/2 inch (1 cm) bigger all around than they are on your sketch to give room to join the pieces together. Sew or glue the pieces together. Ask an adult to help you with the sewing.

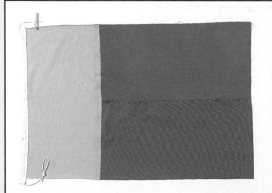

▲ **4.** Thread a piece of string through the tube. Tie a loop in one end of the string and tie a matchstick on the other end.

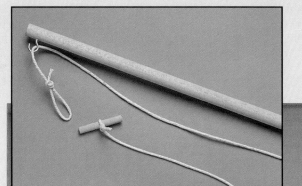

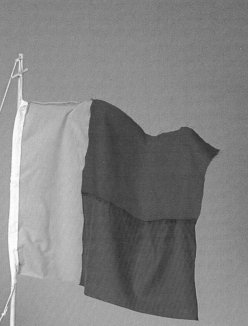

6. Thread the matchstick on the flag through the loop in the halyard. Thread the matchstick on the halyard through the loop on the flag. Now you can hoist your flag.

▲ **5.** Make a flagpole from a piece of wooden dowel. Screw in an eye hook at the top. Glue two blocks of wood to the baseboard with the bottom of the dowel trapped between them. Thread a piece of string through the eye hook. Tie a loop in one and tie a matchstick to the other end to make a halyard.

INTERNATIONAL FLAGS

Most international organizations, such as the International Red Cross and the Olympic Games, have their own flags, which are recognized all over the world. Some famous international flags are shown below.

THE UNITED NATIONS

The United Nations (UN) is an organization with representatives from every country in the world. It came into existence in 1945, after the end of World War II. The emblem on the UN flag is a map of the world surrounded by two olive branches. An olive branch is a symbol of peace. The emblem represents the UN's wish for world peace and cooperation.

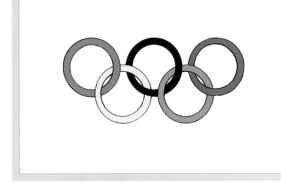

THE OLYMPIC FLAG

The first modern Olympic Games were held in Athens in 1896. The symbol of five rings was devised in 1906, and the flag was first used at the Olympic Games in 1920. The five linked rings represent the five continents of the world united in peace.

THE EUROPEAN COMMUNITY

The flag of the European Community represents the countries of Europe coming together for their mutual benefit. The stars do not represent the individual countries in the Community as is sometimes thought, but harmony and symmetry. The flag was originally, and still is, the flag of the Council of Europe. It was devised in 1955. The EC adopted the flag because they were unable to find a suitable design of their own.

26

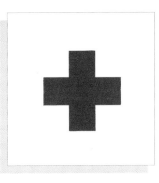

THE INTERNATIONAL RED CROSS AND THE RED CRESCENT

The Red Cross is one of the oldest international organizations. The symbol was devised in 1863 in Geneva, Switzerland, at a conference on the victims of war. It was to be used to mark out hospitals and medical personnel. It was decided that the symbol would be based on the Swiss national flag with the colors reversed. Muslim countries use a similar flag called the Red Crescent.

NORTH ATLANTIC TREATY ORGANIZATION (NATO)

NATO is an organization made up of the military allies around the North Atlantic. The NATO flag has a dark blue background to represent the North Atlantic ocean. The symbol in the center is a compass rose (a drawing of the four points of the compass). It is supposed to point toward peace.

THE ARAB LEAGUE

The Arab League is an organization of countries whose people are mainly Arabic and Muslim. The flag is green (the color of the Islamic religion) with a crescent (a symbol of Islam), a gold chain, and a laurel wreath.

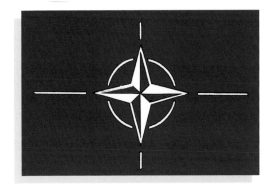

THE ORGANIZATION OF AFRICAN UNITY

The Organization of African Unity represents the interests of all African countries. It was founded in 1963. The flag colors were chosen so that the flag did not look like any of the flags of the member countries, but a combination of all of them. In the center is a small map of Africa.

Using Flags

There are several rules to follow when flying a flag. These rules are not always written down, but are usually observed because flying a flag incorrectly can cause offense to some people. In some countries, and especially in the armed forces, it can be against the law to fly certain flags, such as the national flag, incorrectly.

ON ITS OWN

One important rule is that flags of countries, people, and organizations should not be flown one above the other on the same flagpole. This would mean that one flag was more important than the other. When the flags of two or more countries are flown together, they are flown on separate flagpoles so that they are all at the same height.

THIS WAY UP

It is also important to fly a flag the right way up. A flag flown upside down could look like the flag of another country or a political protest, and flying a flag upside down on a battlefield is a sign of surrender.

However, flying a flag upside down on purpose at sea is a way of signaling for help. The Union Jack is often flown upside down by mistake because it looks symmetrical but it is not.

Correct way up

Upside down

SPECIAL DAYS AND FLAG DAYS

Many countries have special days, such as national or independence days, when the national flag is flown from public buildings. In countries with a king or queen, flags are also flown on their birthdays or on special royal occasions. In some countries anybody is allowed to fly the national flag at any time, but in others people need official permission before they are allowed to fly the national flag at all. Some countries have days called flag days. In the past these were days when charities sold miniature flags to raise money. Today they tend to sell stickers, buttons, or poppies instead.

HOISTING AND FOLDING

Just as much care is needed when hoisting a flag and taking it down as is needed when flying it. Flags should not be allowed to touch the ground while they are being hoisted or lowered. Military flags are always hoisted and folded following a strict, set order.

Below: People waving flags in the streets to greet a member of the royal family who is visiting their town

GLOSSARY

artillery – the guns used by an army.

bunting – strings of small, brightly colored flags hung from buildings on special celebration days.

canton – the name given to each of the four quarters of a flag.

coat of arms – a design of symbols and patterns special to a particular person or family. Originally used as a badge of identity for knights in battle or in tournaments.

draco – a Roman flag in the form of a hollow tube, which billowed out in the wind. The word draco means "dragon."

ensign – a version of a country's national flag flown by a ship.

finial – the top of a flagpole, often carved or decorated.

fly – the outer half of a flag, farthest from the flagpole.

halyard – the long rope used to hoist (pull) the flag up and down the flagpole.

hoist – the half of a flag nearest to the flagpole.

hoist rope – the rope used to attach the flag to the halyards.

jack – a small flag flown at the front of a warship.

legion – a unit of the Roman army, made up of more than 4,000 soldiers.

Morse code – a means of communicating by radio, by tapping out a series of long and short sounds. Invented in 1837.

neutral – a neutral country is one which does not take sides in a war.

obverse – the side of a flag as seen flying from the onlooker's left to right, with the flagpole on the left.

pennant – a long, narrow, triangular flag. Pennant comes from the Latin word, penna, meaning "feather."

regimental colors – the ceremonial flags of a particular army regiment. Used to identify the regiment.

reverse – the side of a flag as seen flying from right to left, with the flagpole on the right.

semaphore – a system of sending messages using two flags held in different positions to stand for numbers and letters of the alphabet.

sleeve – the sleeve of cloth through which the hoist rope is threaded.

standard – the personal flag of a head of state or member of a royal family.

tricolor – a flag with three stripes in different colors.

vexillology – the study of flags.

vexillum – a small standard used by the mounted section of the Roman army.

RESOURCES

PLACES TO WRITE TO OR CALL

You can write to the following for information about flags. Enclose a stamped, self-addressed envelope.

Flag Reseach Center
3 Edgehill Road
Winchester, MA 01890
(617) 729-9410

The Smithsonian Institution
Museum of American History
14th Street and Constitution Avenue
Washington, D.C. 20560
(202) 357-1933

BOOKS TO READ

Alexander, Kent. *Flags.* New York: Mallard Press, 1992.

Brandt, Sue R. *State Flags.* New York: Franklin Watts, 1992.

Crampton, William. *The Complete Guide to Flags.* New York: Gallery Books, 1989.

– – – *Flag.* New York: Knopf, 1989.

Manning, Rosemary. *Heraldry.* Chester Springs, PA: Dufour, 1975.

Mucha, Ludvik. *Webster's Concise Book of Flags and Coats of Arms.* New York: Crescent Books, 1985.

Smith, Whitney. *Flags and Arms Across the World.* New York: McGraw-Hill, 1980.

– – – *Flags Through the Ages and Across the World.* New York: McGraw-Hill, 1975.

INDEX

aircraft 4
Arab League 27
Australia 22

banners 5, 10, 13
battle flags 20
bunting 4

Canada 23
China 5, 23
coats of arms 13-15
code flags 18, 19
communication 4, 5, 17-19
courtesy flags 16

decorated shields 12-13
designing and making a flag 24-5
draco 7
dressing ship 17

ensigns 16, 17
European Community 26

flag days 29
France 22

Germany 23

heraldry 12
hoisting and folding a flag 29

international flags 26-7

jacks 16

Moon landing 4

national flags 5, 10, 16, 21-3, 29
NATO 27
numeral flags 17

Olympic flag 26
Organization of African Unity 27
origin of flags 6

Pakistan 23
pennants 10, 11
pennons 20

Red Crescent 27
Red Cross 27
red flags 5, 19
regimental colors 20, 21
Roman flags 7

semaphore flags 18
shapes and designs 10-11
ships' flags 16-17
solid flags 6
special days 4, 17, 29
sport, flags in 19
standards 7, 13
swallowtail flags 10
symbols and pictures 12, 13

United Kingdom 22
United Nations 26
United States 4, 22

vexillology 7
vexillum 7, 8-9
Viking flags 6

Additional Photographs:
Image Bank/Antonio Rosario 28;
Portfolio Pictures/NASA 5; Rex
Features Ltd 4, 29; TRH/E. Nevill 20;
TRH/M. Roberts 21; ZEFA 17.